May 10, 1991

Happy Birthday, Tanaegh!!

With love,
  Daddy, Mammie, Yvole & Mark

Art Media Series

Creating with Printing Material

Lothar Kampmann

 Van Nostrand Reinhold Company/New York

Illustrations
The work reproduced in the first
part of this book is by students of
the Ruhr Advanced Teachers'
Training College, Dortmund
Section, and by the author. Other
illustrations are from the Pelikan
Archives and the Collection of
the Department of Art
Education of the Ruhr Advanced
Teachers' Training College,
Dortmund Section. A further
source was the Kothe-
Marxmeier school, Trantenroth,
Bochum. The two woodcuts on
p. 4 are from Holzschnitt und
Linolschnitt by Walter
Schurmeyer, Otto Maier Verlag,
Ravensburg.
Sponsored by the Günther
Wagner Pelikan-Werke,
Hannover; and Koh-I-Noor, Inc.,
100 North Street, Bloomsbury,
New Jersey 08804.

German edition © 1968
Otto Maier Verlag, Ravensburg,
Germany.
English Translation Copyright ©
1969
by Litton Educational Publishing, Inc.
Library of Congress Catalog Card
Number 74-83387. ISBN 0-442-11359-5
Printed and bound in Italy
Published in the United States of
America by Van Nostrand
Reinhold Company,
450 West 33rd Street,
New York, N.Y. 10001.

16 15 14 13 12 11 10 9 8 7 6 5 4 3 2

Foreword

Books are products of the printer's art. This has long ceased to be a novelty; we take it for granted that books as well as newspapers and works of art are printed, and that literary as well as educational material is thus made accessible to the general public. We are aware that printing has contributed to the spread of popular education. But perhaps we do not realise what an important historical event the invention of printing was: it was one of the outstanding achievements that separate the Middle Ages from the present day.

Our newspapers originated in the hand-printed handbills of the late Middle Ages which carried the news to the public. In the fifteenth century the book of books, the Bible, became the first of a flood of printed books that has all but engulfed us. Even earlier, Dürer of Nuremberg was making woodcuts and copper engravings. Thus our modern art is really very ancient. Of course, the tedious cutting of individual types in boxwood blocks has long given way to the quicker process of the typesetting machine, and filmsetting machines will soon replace the cast types.

In spite of the respectable history of printing as a legitimate artistic activity, for centuries the woodcut, wood engraving, copper engraving and steel engraving were considered only minor arts suited perhaps to reproducing the paintings of the masters for the masses. Not until the age of art nouveau and expressionism were the graphic processes finally accorded an important place in the sphere of the visual arts. But since then artistic printing has gone far beyond its original function of duplication and reproduction. These new developments are the subject of this book.

Originally there were only two basic art-printing techniques, which were sufficient to achieve perfect duplication: relief printing and intaglio printing. Printing ink was the only material, and was found perfectly adequate. It consisted, as it still does, basically of fine varnish and fine soot, thoroughly ground together into a paste. But the new age has invented new techniques: lithography, zincography, offset printing and silkscreen printing. Each new technique requires its own printing inks, and the new colours tempt artists to new experiments. The ability to duplicate a picture cut, engraved, traced or drawn on a block is still a distinctive property of the various printing techniques. But it is by no means the only important property any longer. The modern artist has come to realize the possibilities of expression inherent in the art of printing and attempts to explore them fully.

'St Christopher'. Woodcut, 1423

Franz Marc: 'Tiger'. Woodcut

Printing techniques

Not every art in the printer's repertoire is suitable for schools, which usually lack professional equipment. On the other hand, printing in schools certainly need not be restricted to black and white. Modern techniques of colour printing have extended it into an immensely lively, gay art, full of variety and interest. The special attraction of printing in school is perhaps its very imperfections, and the improvisation it demands.

With the invention of linoleum, printing in schools became practical. Woodcuts require a strong, practised hand, which one cannot expect young children to have. But linoleum blocks are softer and comparatively cheap. A further convenience was the development of a new colour 'paste' which children can work with without damaging their clothes beyond repair — water-soluble block-printing ink. This special ink, linoleum and cutting tools that can be inserted in a penholder, are all that is needed for printing in school. Finally, the development of miniature printing presses has made etching possible in schools. The cheap zinc plate has taken the place of the expensive copper plate. Over the years the basic techniques have been extended and varied; new ones have been added. Many a technique reached the school from the artist's studio; and conversely, the artist has sometimes benefited from methods employed in art education. Nevertheless, printing has not yet achieved as important a role in schools as it could. This book is intended to show what can be done and how the many printing techniques can be applied.

Printing can be either extremely simple or extremely complicated — and thus it can be a worthwhile pursuit from a child's fourth year onwards, throughout his whole life. So let us start with the very basis of the art of printing. What does 'printing', 'copying', involve? There must always be an object with which to print, and another object to receive the print. But the print would leave no trace unless a third component is added: a dyeing or tracing substance which is transferred from the first object to the second.

Thus, three items are necessary with every type of process:

1. The block, the plate or the stamp — that is, the ink carrier. It is prepared to take up a colour substance.
2. The printer's ink, colour substance or other printing material with which the block is inked.
3. The object suitable for receiving the print.

It starts with fingermarks

We see our children's first printing achievements on wallpaper and windowpanes, in magazines and books: their fingermarks. They are greasy or black with dirt. Sometimes jam makes them coloured. They may be annoying to the housewife, but technically they are genuine products of printing.

The young artist merely has to be guided on to the right lines.

Dirt and jam make way to colour. The little cups of the poster-paint box are ideal as the first inking pads. Since the tip of the thumb and the fingertips are of different sizes, we already have various sizes of block available for finger printing.

This is not by any means a technique only for infants' schools. Masters as eminent as Pablo Picasso have repeatedly made use of fingerprinting in lithography.

Rewarding compositions are possible with white (poster white) on black, or with black (block-print-

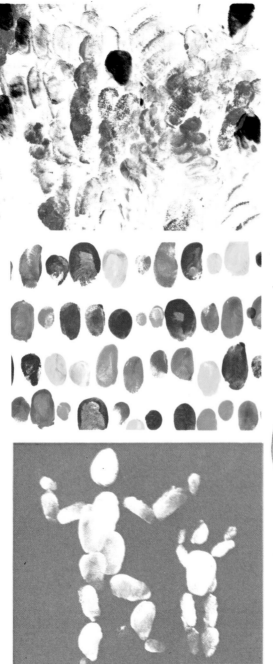

ing ink) on white. Other colour combinations are obviously also possible.

The whole hand, too, is a suitable block. The print of a single hand can be extended with a print of the edge of the hand, the single whole fingers, or the fingertips. Or 'many hands' are used for printing. Such handprints are known from the very early days of man. Neanderthal and Lascaux man used earth-coloured handprints in their cave paintings. One can rightly regard the fingerprint as the beginning of printing both for the individual and for the human race.

Arrangement and play: printing with coloured stamps

A step further brings us to printing with coloured stamps. Even the youngest children can do this, arranging the patterns repetitively or centrally.

The possibilities for invention are wide. Corks of various sizes are inked and printed on paper. The main task is to find methods of arrangement.

Such cork stamps can be made more elaborate by cutting and notching them. They can be halved or quartered lengthwise. It must be

remembered that it takes a very sharp knife to cut cork, and this can be a hazard to small hands. It is better for the teacher to do the cutting.

Potato printing is less dangerous, since potato is easy to cut and the knife need not be sharp. This technique is, therefore, particularly suitable for primary schools. Also,

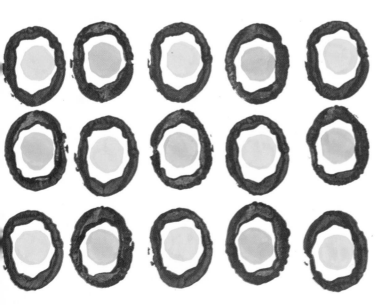

9

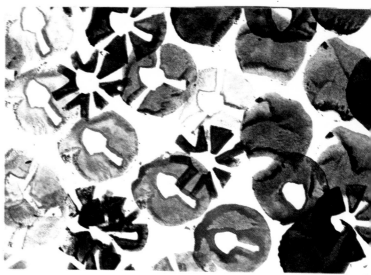

potato is naturally moist; this is an advantage in both the inking process and the printing process, for which poster paints are used.

Potato printing is customarily used only decoratively, for so-called 'carpet or pattern printing'. However, the arrangement of various elements in a design can be complicated enough to interest even older children, since the problems involve composition as well as technique.

10

Cardboard offers many opportunities

Potato printing should be followed by cardboard printing. Start with a print of the edge of a sheet of cardboard (a technique which produces good results also in schools for retarded children). This requires cardboard strips or rectangles of the strongest possible cardboard. The edge is inked and printed in poster paints, block-printing ink, indian ink, or ordinary ink.

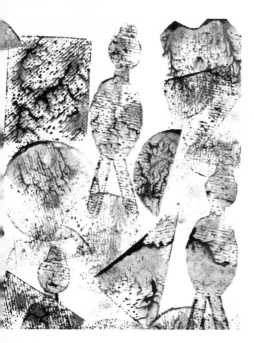

Since cardboard strips are flexible, curves can be printed with them. Lastly, the cardboard sheets themselves can be used.
Alternate sheet and edge printing is the next stage.

The first step towards relief printing

Another cardboard technique will serve as introduction to the process of relief printing. Up till now each piece of cardboard has been printed repeatedly on its own. Now the various pieces are arranged and pasted on a cardboard support. Space is left between the various pieces. The printing roller

and block-printing ink enter the scene here for the first time (see p. 17). We have made our first relief block, which must be generously inked with the roller. A sheet of absorbent paper is placed on top and printed well. It is generally best to rub the sheet on the block with a spoon handle or a paper knife. If you have a sturdy hand-printing roller, you will produce a print of superior quality.

Naturally, you can go a step further and cut little figures out of the cardboard and stick them on the cardboard support in the desired arrangement.

Building up a print

An interesting advance is the building up of a print. In our example three 'pictures' were prepared: a background, a middle distance and a foreground.

The middle distance was printed over the background, and the foreground over the combined middle

distance and background.

This method becomes even more interesting when the foreground, middle distance and background are shifted in various ways. There is the additional opportunity of expanding each individual block by adding new picture elements. Thus a completely new picture can be

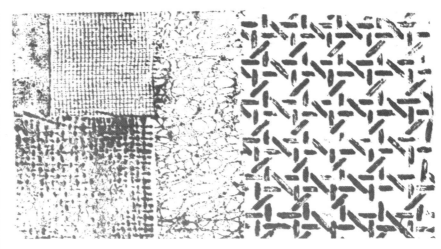

produced during each printing run.

Printing with existing materials

We have still to learn much before we can take up the 'artistic' printing techniques such as the linocut, woodcut and etching. We were able to print with the cork as we found it. There are quite a number of other materials which can be used for printing simply by inking them: wire-mesh, coarse fabric, cord, curtain lace, etc. They can be arranged and pasted down on some support, like the pieces of cardboard, and printed. With this 'material printing', care must be taken to use, if possible, only materials of about the same height on the block. Otherwise there is a risk of tearing the paper during rubbing or printing.

A special technique has developed from this 'material printing': cord printing. Cord of the same thickness can be laid out to your own designs and glued to the base. When you print them, these structures produce quite distinctive patterns.

And now a printing method for patient people: printing with matchsticks. We make use of the fact that matches are generally of the same thickness. Only used matches are employed, since the heads would interfere with the printing.

For larger formats boards from wooden crates are handy; they are inked and printed.

These last few techniques are already typical 'relief' techniques — that is, everything that is to make an impression has to be raised on the block. The surfaces take up the ink and transfer it to the printing material.

Here the use of block-printing ink is recommended; it is evenly applied with the printing roller. The printing ink is squeezed on a sheet of glass and transferred to the block with a roller. Those who try to apply the printing ink with a brush will find that it does not work.

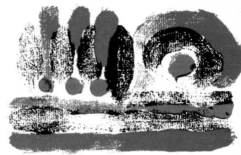

Monotype: the simplest surface-printing technique

We just mentioned block-printing ink. You can print with it even without a printing block. Such printing techniques are intermediate between relief and intaglio printing, and we can classify them under the heading of surface printing.

The easiest surface-printing technique is monotype. This 'one-time' printing method can be either simple or extremely complicated. The simplest form is illustrated here. Block-printing ink is applied to a sheet of glass with a brush. The right amount of ink must be found by trial and error. If the application is too generous, the print will have ugly, thick colour blotches; if too little ink is used the print may be dull and lifeless. The

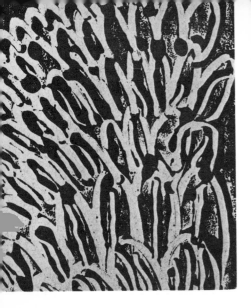

printing paper is placed over the brush drawing, squeezed down with the palm of the hand, and carefully peeled off the glass.

You can elaborate on this technique. Instead of applying block-printing ink with a brush, roll it evenly on the whole of the glass sheet. Now draw on this uniformly inked surface with the brush handle or a small stick. The tracings will appear as white lines in the print. We use the terms 'white', 'white line', etc., even though you may be using coloured paper to print on, as was done with many of the prints illustrated here.

Poster tempera paint is also suited for monotype with a glass sheet. Here a wide range of the most varied colours is available. However, you must work quickly:

a

b

poster paint dries more rapidly than block-printing ink.

You can produce an interesting effect by wiping the drawing with a damp rag (p. 18,a).

Finally, you can use a razor blade to scrape away colour or clear larger areas by pushing the blade sideways (p. 18,b).

However, the most reliable method of obtaining a black-and-white or light-dark monotype is the scrap-of-paper technique of placing torn or cut scraps of paper on the inked surface before printing. Where the paper covers the surface, bright patches will appear in the print.

When the scraps of paper are removed from the sheet of glass after printing, a second print can be made from the 'block'. The result will be a misty grey effect.

The combination of all the possibilities on the same sheet is particularly interesting. In addition,

paint can be applied to the pieces
of paper with a brush.

The crowning achievement of
monotype is multiplate monotype,
where each colour has its own
sheet of glass and all colours are
printed one on top of the other.

After transfer monotypes let us go
on to the print-through process,
the simplicity of which is unsur-

passed. Its possibilities are limited, but you ought to know how to make the best of it. The basic process is as follows. The glass sheet is inked evenly and very thinly with a roller. The paper to be printed on is placed on this thin film of ink.

The moisture of the ink makes it slightly adhesive. You can now draw on the paper with a pencil or a ball-point. The drawing is printed through; that is, the printing paper takes up printing ink from the glass on its back, side-reversed.

The intriguing quality of this technique is its chance results. They make the harsh lines of the pencil or ball-point stroke into something picturesque. You can enhance this effect by means of grey areas, which you can print through in addition to the already existing lines by rubbing with a finger. It is best to try it in advance. Even a light stroke with the ball of the thumb over the paper on the plate produces a soft, wide stroke of grey.

The printing-through process, as well as monotype with various coloured plates that print successively, is an interesting way of expanding your practical knowledge.

Since the glass plate is already inked, let us have a little fun. Splash a few drops of water on the plate, place the paper on top for printing, and print it down by hand or roll it firmly down with a clean printing roller. The results are sometimes stimulating enough to suggest an entirely new design. But you must not be deceived into thinking that the attractive accidental effect is the result of your

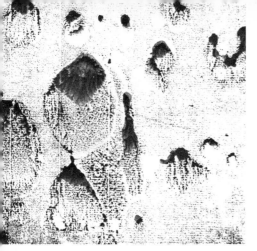

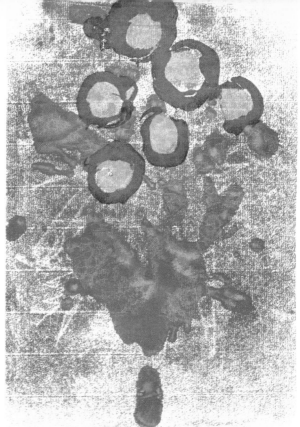

own powers of imagination. As an existing element, the accidental effect may present a new creative challenge. For example, a colour monotype can be inserted into such an accidental pattern. In our picture, various coloured inkspots were distributed on the glass plate, then the paper was pressed down with the roller.

Finally, we must say something about the roller. This tool, too, can be more than an ink carrier or substitute for a printing press. You can work directly on the paper with the roller and block-printing ink. All you have to do is to try it. Very useful creative results can be obtained with roller-printing, particularly when you use different printing inks.

22

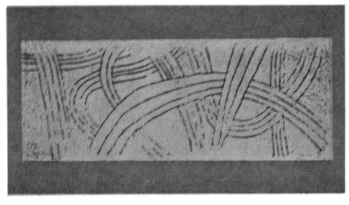

First attempts with lino: the white-line print

It is now time to talk about true 'prints', starting with lino prints. Let us begin with the white-line print.

A little detour must be mentioned here. If you draw firm lines on fairly thick soft cardboard with a strong knitting needle, the needle will trace impressions. If the cardboard surface is now inked, a print on paper will produce white lines. Do the same with lino, but cut lines into it with a lino-cutter's knife. The lines do not take up ink. Always cut with the knife *away from your hand* to avoid injury.

It is advisable to make your first attempts on small pieces of lino. Mistakes are easily made, and if you spoil a large piece right at the beginning, you lose all the fun you might get from it. Small pieces of lino scrap, which you can cut to size, can be obtained from shops

selling wallpaper and floor coverings. You can start by arranging these scraps on a support as in the cardboard-printing method (see p. 12), fixing them with adhesive; then cutting out the white lines. The next step must be the reversal of this process: instead of the white line, the positive print provides the pattern.

Lino shape printing

An intermediate form is the 'white-patch' print. This produces false ribs, which divide the patches from each other. It represents the development of the white-line into the white-patch cut.

Carry on with this process, except that you now produce the white line on the lino with a brush dipped in poster white. This simplifies your task: the white line must remain, the rest of the lino must be cut away.

The result is the lino shape print. The narrow cutting knives used to make lines are replaced by broad gauges to scoop out large areas.

Two basic approaches are pos-

sible: you can make such clean cuts that only the ribs remain or you can graphically solve the problem of the empty spaces between the ribs by leaving bits of lino in them to produce delicate lines in the print.

You now have various types of block that you can combine: white-line cut and shape cut. Repeat printing offers new possibilities.

Stamping dies as blocks

A most effective, though perhaps uncommon version of lino cutting must not be ignored: printing with stamping dies. For this you need hollow punches in various sizes to punch holes in the lino. The process is quite simple. Place the lino on a firm support and position the hollow punch. A firm blow with a hammer on the hollow punch and you will have a hole.

The punched discs of lino can in turn be arranged and printed, like

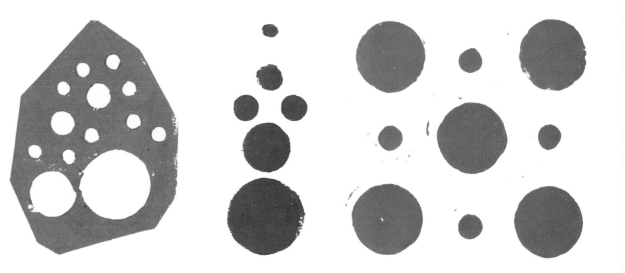

pieces of cardboard.
When you have collected enough scraps from the punching, you can print in two or three colours by superimposition. Lastly, the combination of negative punch holes and positive stamped shapes can produce good results.

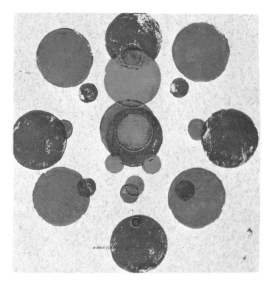

Printing in several colours with lino

You have now reached the stage of printing in several colours with lino.

The simplest way of printing in colour is to ink the cut shapes successively with the different inks

and offset the block slightly each time it is printed.

The next basic possibility consists in printing coloured areas with a blank lino block, and overprinting them with an existing lino cut, or

printing various part blocks before printing the lino cut. This printing of coloured areas is the simple forerunner of real multicolour printing.

One printing element after the other is inked with different colours and printed on the paper. The picture gradually builds up — an additive process, which can be expanded at will.

Up till now, your printing has been carefree and uninhibited.

With all additive, arranging, build-up printing processes the final result remains uncertain until the last element has been printed down. Conditions are different with the multiplate print. The first requirement here is the multi-coloured layout, which is best done in poster paints or poster tempera paints. When choosing your colours, make sure that all the tones in the design are available in printing colours, to avoid the inevitable disappointment if the colour effect of the printed sheet differs greatly from that of the design. The coloured shapes must be clearly outlined against one another, as printing does not allow gradual transitions.

First the colour separations are made. For this purpose place white tracing paper (used by architects) on the design, 'extracting' one colour after the other. In our ex-

ample four colour separations are obtained. For marking the colour separations felt-tipped pens are best: they do not crinkle the paper as water colours do.

All the lines and shapes in one colour each are now recorded on the sheets of tracing paper. Depending on the number of colours involved they are transferred to the prepared, same-sized lino blocks by means of carbon paper. The blocks are now cut and printed one after the other. Since you have four plates at your disposal you will find it interesting to change the colours around or replace them with new ones. This sometimes leads to instructive modifications of the original design.

If the printing is not done carefully, the blocks will be wrongly superimposed. Of course, such displacements can be introduced

deliberately in order to obtain special effects.

But there comes a stage when you have made enough prints and tried out enough variations. Things become boring, and the blocks are forgotten. Perhaps they are even thrown away. This would be a pity, because they still offer a number of possible printing techniques.

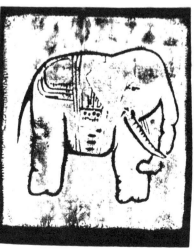

Discarded printing blocks still have their uses

There is, for instance, the adhesive-blind-printing method. The block is 'inked' with white paste (the water-soluble kind commonly used in schools and libraries) instead of with printing inks. An adhesive print is produced on the paper. As soon as the 'picture' is dry it can be covered with black india ink or ordinary black ink. As soon as this has become dry, the adhesive is washed off under the water tap.

The areas or lines that were formerly printed black are now white against the inked background.

Or you can dust the still-wet adhesive with gold bronze. The most striking effect is of course obtained on black, dark-blue, or dark-green paper. Too garish? Perhaps a little questionable — there is no quarrelling about tastes — but you need not be too timid.

The two following further possibilities take advantage of the relief character of the lino-cut. Soak the printing paper in a water bath for five minutes. Remove surplus water between sheets of cloth or absorbent paper, and place the paper on the printing block. The paper, which is now pliant and soft, is pressed into the lino relief with the thumb and the heel of the hand so that it acquires the same relief structure as the lino block. It is best to allow the paper to dry on the lino before it is peeled off. Lastly, the dry relief surface can be inked with the roller.

The same method is of course suitable for the cardboard printing block. Also, if you wish you can 'ink' your lino-cut with a little oil and pour plaster of Paris on top. This will give you a negative plaster cast.

However, eventually there is absolutely nothing more to do with the lino block, no matter how much

you rack your brains. Or is there?
There always remains the possibility of cutting up the lino block
and recombining the various parts
in new compositional arrangements, which can again be printed
— black and white, coloured, on
supports printed in colour, on
coloured paper — there is no end
to it.

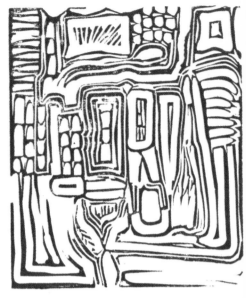

In calico printing the process of duplication becomes a meaningful element of design. All the relief-printing techniques described so far are suitable. The paper is merely replaced by fabric. Special block-printing inks for calico are available. They are applied with a roller. Our example shows an oil print.

A few notes on woodcutting

To complete our description of basic techniques, the woodcut must be briefly mentioned. Whatever we have said about lino-cutting applies also to wood — the only difference is that wood (it should be hardwood) is more difficult to work and more expensive.

If the pupils have been introduced to carpentry tools, woodcutting on crate boards will probably be feasible in the upper grades. Apple-crates and orange-crates can be cheaply obtained from a fruit merchant. This kind of wood can be worked fairly effectively with the gouge.

The prints are of course rather rough. But perhaps that is their special appeal.

phenomenon accounts for our interest in this material.

Apply a varnish thinner to the expanded polystyrene with a coarse brush. The material will immediately dissolve under the stippling or stroking touch of the brush, as if the thinner was eating into it. This results in a printing block that almost automatically has an interesting structure.

Printing with expanded polystyrene

Polystyrene, a white, extremely light, foamy plastic, is very well known as a packing and display material. It is sold in the form of plates of various thicknesses. Of course it can be cut or broken, and the pieces can be used for printing. But it also has a special property. If you have ever tried to glue expanded polystyrene with a standard household cement, you may have found that the cement contained a solvent that dissolved the expanded polystyrene. This

What is intaglio printing?

From the discussion of surface and relief printing we are now passing on to intaglio printing. In this technique impressions are made in the surface of the printing block, and the impressions are filled with printing ink. The ink is then removed from the intact surfaces — which were the ink carriers in relief printing. The printing paper is moistened to make it pliable, placed on the block, and covered with a sheet of felt. Printing block, paper, and sheet of felt are now rolled through the intaglio-plate press. The pliable paper, forced into the ink-filled impressions in the plate under high pressure, takes up some of the ink. For this process an intaglio-plate press is almost essential.

35

A preliminary exercise for this technique is the cardboard-scratch print. Instead of applying the ink with a roller, rub it into the cardboard vigorously with a piece of cloth. This fills the scratch drawing and at the same time keeps the ink off the surface of the cardboard. This is followed by printing as previously described.

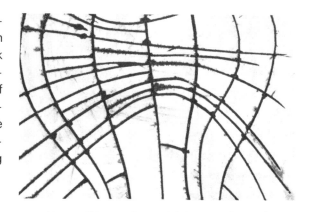

The lino white-line print is also suitable for teaching the principle of this technique. However, if the lino block is used for intaglio printing the cuts must be very fine or they will take up too much ink.

Drypoint, etching and aquatint

After such preliminary exercises we can go on to etching. The simplest form is the drypoint method. A zinc plate with a surface as shiny and flawless as possible, an etching needle, and copperplate ink are necessary for this method.

With even pressure the etching needle leaves glistening traces, which are inked by rubbing them with a piece of cloth or the ball of the thumb. The strong pressure of the etching or copperplate press

presses the softened paper into the fine lines; the paper takes up the ink from these lines.

A little ink can be deliberately left on the surface of the plate. If a slight tint is desired in the print, just a trace of ink, no more, is left on the plate. The printer will learn this by trial and error.

But you can do more than just trace lines with drypoint. Very fine narrow or wide hatching produces a half-tone effect.

You can also ink the surface in colour, provided you use oil inks.

The process about to be introduced is called etching.

Everybody knows that hydrochloric acid attacks zinc. However, the zinc plate is to be attacked only where desired. It must, therefore, first be protected against the acid. You can do this best by covering it with a mixture of beeswax and asphalt varnish. In the past every copperplate engraver

The thoroughly cleaned, shiny zinc plate is coated thinly but completely with this asphalt varnish. It is very important that the edges and the back of the plate also be covered with the varnish. After about half an hour the varnish is thoroughly dry, hard and no longer tacky. The drawing is traced with the etching needle in the zinc plate through the varnish film. The physical effort required is less than with drypoint. After the etching patterns have been traced in the film, the whole plate is placed in a shallow glass or plastic dish containing diluted acid, which immediately begins to bite into the traced lines and any unprotected surface of the zinc. It is up to the printer how long he leaves the plate in the acid. He will learn by experience: at a certain dilution of the acid certain line widths and depths are produced within a certain time. The longer the acid is allowed to act, the deeper it will bite into the zinc. A deep line takes up much ink and produces a line in more saturated colours during printing. Obviously, it will also become coarser in certain circumstances, for the acid penetrates not only downwards, but also sideways. After the etching the varnish is removed from the plate with turpentine; then the plate can be rubbed with ink and printed.

and etcher concocted his own special mixture. Today we can buy stopping-out varnish, or asphalt cones made with similar ingredients.

You can also paint on the zinc plate with asphalt varnish, thus covering precise areas of your choice. To the printer this means that he has to think in opposites. For what he has painted with the varnish will in the print remain white. It is a kind of negative design. The etched portions print half-tone areas of delicate tint.

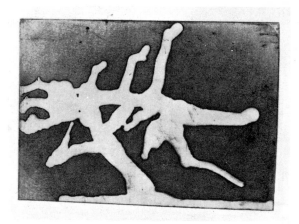

In order to obtain areas of different tint strengths, you have to repeat the etching process twice or three times in separate stages. Naturally, whatever features are to remain in the condition they have already reached must be protected with varnish when the plate is redipped in acid.

Now drypoint and etching can be combined.

Colophony is a yellow, brittle resin well known to those who study the violin. It can be crushed to powder and melted. But it does not react with acids. We take advantage of this in a special variant of etching called aquatint.

Colophony is crushed and poured into a small gauze bag. The zinc plate is dusted with this bag, but not too liberally. The plate is gently heated. At this stage seconds are decisive. You have to wait for the moment at which the colophony begins to melt. Too much heat, or too long over the heat, and the colophony will melt all over the plate. You want the granules to melt separately on to the support without running together. Etching can now begin. In the print a fine stipple effect is the result.

Naturally you can develop individual little plates with this technique, too, or cut up a large zinc plate in order to compose with the various parts on the block.

This does not mean by any means exhaust all the printing methods. However, as far as school is concerned, not much more can be done with basic techniques. Certainly many an art teacher will know of special methods for which he has prepared his students. In this book, however, only methods that are generally suitable can be outlined.

or stout cardboard with household cement directly from the tube. The cement should be the colourless quick-drying kind. The strokes of cement make ridges on the block. When they are dry, the block can be inked and printed as in any other relief-printing method.

Imitation veneers on adhesive-backed plastic sheets can be used to make blocks. Cut out little figures with a pair of scissors and

Experiments with household cement and plastic sheets

We must not forget two special printing processes which are striking, yet very simple and practicable. One is a kind of relief, the other a kind of intaglio printing. The relief block should be prepared as follows. Make a drawing on lino

stick them down on a lino, zinc or celluloid plate, which should be as thin as possible. The prepared block is then rubbed in one or several colours. Oil inks are best for this purpose. In this method the cut edges do the printing. All areas are wiped with a rag and cleaned to a greater or lesser degree according to the effect desired. Printing is carried out in the intaglio-plate press.

The printing techniques leave wide scope for experimenting; much is still left to the inventive mind. Combinations of various techniques will be very fruitful. All that is necessary is patience. Many a method will not yield success at the very first attempt. This must not discourage you — just try again. Often the techniques are too complicated to succeed the very first time.

Printing as a school activity

A few educational considerations

Compared with drawing and painting, printing is more technical and less spontaneous, except for finger-printing and handprinting. In general, printing lacks the dynamic movement and activity of the free strokes of pencil or brush. However, children like printing every bit as much as they like scribbling and painting. All you have to do is to give them stamps and an ink pad. The repetitive arrangement of patches of any kind gives them great pleasure, and can be very educational.

The great variety of the different techniques makes it possible always to go from the simple to the complicated, from the familiar to the new. Naturally one starts with fingerprinting and handprinting. Here the only technical feature, apart from the printing process as such, is the inking. Printing with corks handed out by the teacher accustoms the child to the use of the first tools. In potato printing he learns how he can give these tools the shapes he wants. He acquires the technical ability to make stamps, whether the raw material is cork, india rubber or lino. During material printing he experiences the 'stampability' of various objects in his environment and thus learns new forms and possibilities of combining forms. He now progresses from the cardboard to the lino block, and on the block that was inked in black he realizes, in passing as it was, the effect of monotype.

If the pupil masters these methods, he will have no difficulties in understanding the subsequent techniques. This understanding, of course, is essential, since all printing is a translation of pictorial or graphic ideas into mechanical processes.

The print on paper is always the image of previous pictorial composition. (We are ignoring accidental phenomena, since they are completely beyond control.) Pictorial composition in any art form is orderly arrangement on a surface and in space, and this arrangement of areas, points of gravity and of concentration, colours and brightness values is the preliminary step to artistic printing. However, all genuine printing methods are processes of *indirect* pictorial composition. The printer must be fully conscious of what he is doing to obtain the effects he wants, and this is what makes printing a superlative learning and teaching method. The additive build-up techniques are especially suitable for experiencing and practising pictorial arrangement, because the printing block or blocks have their own individual arrangements, and the area-distributing and the colour-distributing steps that lead to the finished print are actually arrangements of arrangements.

We give below a few examples of formal work sequences with which 'pictorial arrangement' can be brought home to the child through his own activities. Our examples are chosen more for their logical work sequence than for their subject content. Any subject can be developed in an orderly fashion.

1. White-line cut. Lines are arranged on top of and behind one another as in a landscape in which a plain, hills, peaks and mountain ranges are spaced in depth.

a. The task is to progress from the static base line to more and more dynamic lines as we move to the top of the picture. Intersections are desirable.

b. The lino block is cut vertically

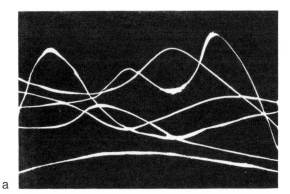

a

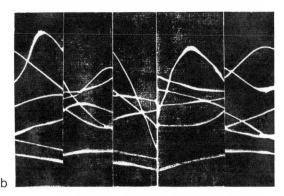

b

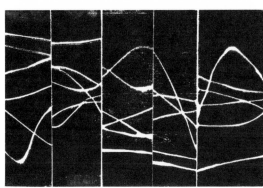

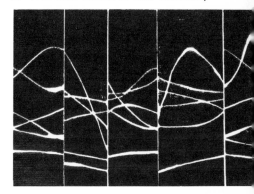

into four or five parts, rearranged, and printed again. This reveals that many a new arrangement is decidedly better than the original design. The lines, of course, now end in the 'wrong' places.

c. The best arrangement is fixed on a sheet of cardboard. The flow of the lines is re-established by re-connecting them where they are interrupted by the cuts.

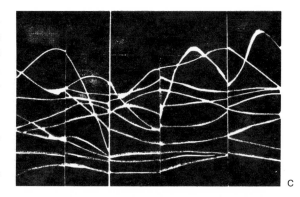

c

d

d. The white-line cut is converted into a shape cut by gouging out the mass.

The white-line cut on its own is not an outstanding pictorial achievement. It is quickly designed and cut. After the third print the children find it very boring. The creative activity consists in the design. The subsequent development to the printing stage is merely a non-artistic, technical process. Duplication itself has no creative value at all. It is therefore always advisable to let the white-line cut become the starting point for further creative work. We have been able to show clearly how a given cut can be 'composed' more effectively, how something that began as a simple design can be organically enlarged and finally technically perfected. It is never enough to let the child do only what he could learn without a teacher. Every task must be made into a problem of creativeness for the pupil. This is the only chance to prevent boredom in the intelligent child and indifference in the others.

2. Printing with the potato stamp. An oblong, a square and a triangle are provided. Each element must be given a tone of the earth-colour series.

a. These elements are arranged alternately in rows and in a solid area.

b. The same elements are used for 'constructional printing', in the literal sense, so that silhouettes of cities are produced. These silhouettes are in turn arranged in rows one above the other.

c. The elements are arranged centrally, in concentric rings around a focal point. Secondary subject: a marketplace around which rows of houses have grown. Streets may radiate from the marketplace.

d. The elements are to be arranged formally, concentrically.

Potato printing still has something of the nursery school about it. This makes one tend to use it mainly for producing decorative paper. In the long run this is a purely mechanical effort in which the child cannot see any sense. However, if this most elementary technique is subordinated to a more ambitious aim of composition, potato printing can teach the child a great deal.

Here we are concerned with patterned arrangements leading from a mechanical arrangement to one that represents concrete objects, and further to a central conceptual order, and finally to a formally central order. The transitions become clear; the principal of order is there for all to see. No change takes place in the technique. It is obvious that these motifs can be varied at any time, in their elements, colours, format and principle of arrangement.

3. Material printing. The subject is the structure of wood.

a. Well-grained pieces of wood are composed into a solid pictorial structure by means of printing.

b. The line structure of the grain is freely converted into cord print.

c. The cord print is converted into an adhesive (blind) print. This is followed by the wash-off technique with india ink (p. 31).

d. The same composition is painted in lines in earth paints, and repeated in household cement over the paint. Finally the whole is washed under water.

We have been exploring a single creative principle here. The important point has been the nature of flow lines, which we can also observe in water. This subject was pursued through various techniques.

Some subjects do not naturally claim the child's interest. Nevertheless their creative content may be so valuable that it is worth trying to present them to the child in an interesting manner. This means that a change of technique that involves some entirely new feature must be introduced.

All the printing techniques, and the many different ways of developing them, have a single aim: to familiarize the child, the pupil, with the possibilities of creative order. In teaching we cannot achieve much without guidance. This guidance is quite legitimate; after all the aim is to teach the pupil to use his knowledge and facilities independently, to make his own decisions. In creative teaching, purposive teaching and learning methods will always alternate with decisions freely arrived at by the child and experimental play.

We show below a number of prints done by schoolchildren in various printing techniques.

'Indian Chief' (boy, 6). Fingerprint with poster paints. The children were told to ink the paper in their favourite colour before printing. For technique, see p. 7.

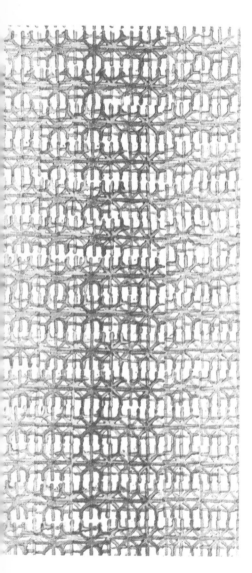

Stamp print with block-printing ink, in colour (girl, 15). The stamps were cut in india rubber. The first print is strongly coloured, the subsequent ones become progressively lighter.

Stamp print with india rubber and block-printing ink (girl, 14).

See also p. 8.

'Church' (boy, 11). Cork print with water colours. For technique, see p. 8.

'Aquarium'. Cork print on black paper.

'Flowers and Grass' (girl, 12). Stamp print with the edge of a sheet of cardboard, a small cork and water colours.

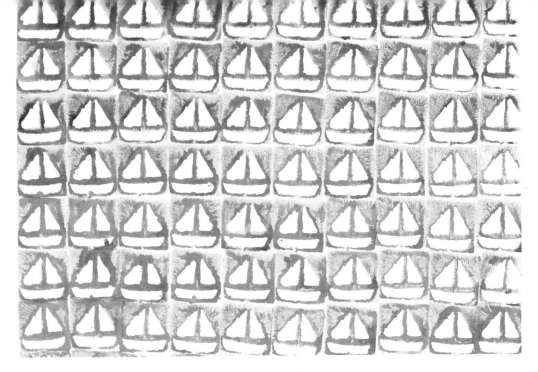

Paper for a book cover (girl, 12). Potato stamp and water colour.

The block was the end of a wooden bar. Poster paint (girl, 10).

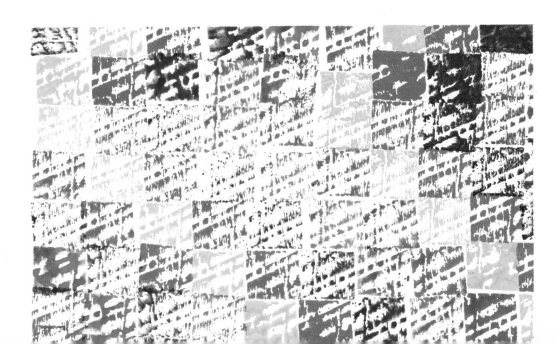

Material print (girl, 13). Pressed
grass ears were carefully inked
with a roller and lino-printing ink
and printed on heavy cartridge
paper.

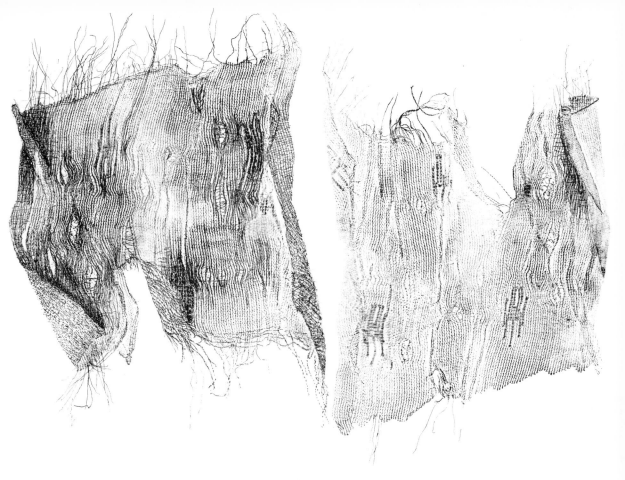

Material print (girl, 14). A piece of butter muslin, inked with block-printing ink and printed.

Decorative material print (girl, 12). Barberry leaves and block-printing ink.

Water-colour print (girl, 13). The original was painted in thick poster paints straight on a plastic tabletop. This was covered with paper, which took up the picture. For technique, see p. 17.

56

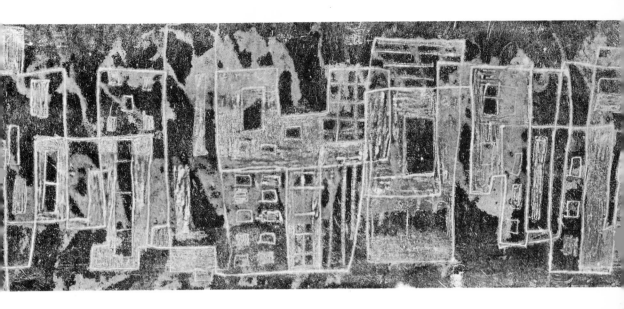

'Garland of Houses' (boy, 14).
Negative monotype: that is, a print
of the inked support, after the first
original had been peeled off according to the printing-through
method. For technique, see p. 21.

'Woodland Path' (girl, 15). A
monotype in which the mirror-
reversed picture was painted with
a brush and stippled. For technique, see p. 17.

'Two Figures' (girl, 16). Paper print of patterns cut out of cartridge paper. Water colours. For technique, see p. 20.

A negative monotype with paper patterns (boy, 12). The patterns were arranged on the inked plate, rolled down with paper, and removed from the plate. Then the final print was made. The paper had removed most of the ink from the plate. (Compare with thread monotypes, p. 59.)

For technique, see p. 19.

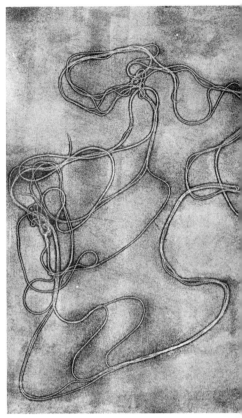

A combination of direct and indirect printing-through (boy, 10). The black lines were produced directly (see p. 21). Then the sheet was again placed on the sheet of glass and pressed down with the roller.

Thread monotype (girl, 11). A simple procedure: a thread is placed on the inked surface. This is covered with a sheet of paper and printed. The thread is now removed from the plate, having taken up ink from where it had been. Hence the white thread line after repeated printing.

'Bicycles Outside the Playground', (boy, 14). Print-through monotype. This is not how they should be left, blocking the entrance.

'Grey Cat' (boy, 7). Print-through drawing.

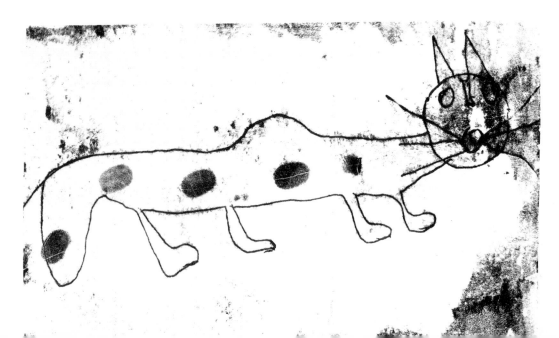

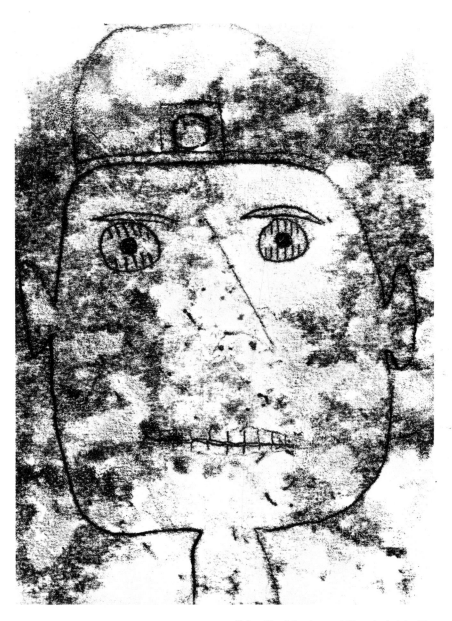

'My Daddy is a Miner' (girl, 9).
Print-through from a glass plate.
All accidental features are re-
produced.

'Industrial Landscape' (boy, 15).
Two-colour roller print; brown and
black block-printing ink. For technique, see p. 22.

A special version of roller printing (girl, 13). It has much in common with the rubbing-through or rubbing-off method. The paper patterns are arranged on the table, covered with a sheet of paper, and pressed down with the printing roller. The patterns underneath press through, taking up more ink than the surrounding paper.

'Many Gearwheels' (boy, 10). White-line lino cut. This boy had only black block-printing ink to work with, but one can easily imagine the effect of various colours or of printing on a coloured paper. The same block was printed contiguously four times.

64

Teamwork (boys and girls, 12).
Four children in turn printed their
lino-cut subjects on grey paper
(see also p. 29).

'Owl Seizing its Prey'. Lino-cut.

Lino-cut (girl, 12). 'After a day's work, only Mummy has to carry on.'

'In Port' (boy, 11). Grey-tone lino-cut.

'Composition with Houses' (boy, 15). Lino-cut on paper inked in red.

Facing page:
'View of the Town through Scaffolding' (boy, 14). A lino-cut in which shape and white-line printing are combined.

'Still Life' (girl, 16). Multicolour
lino-cut. For technique, see p. 30.

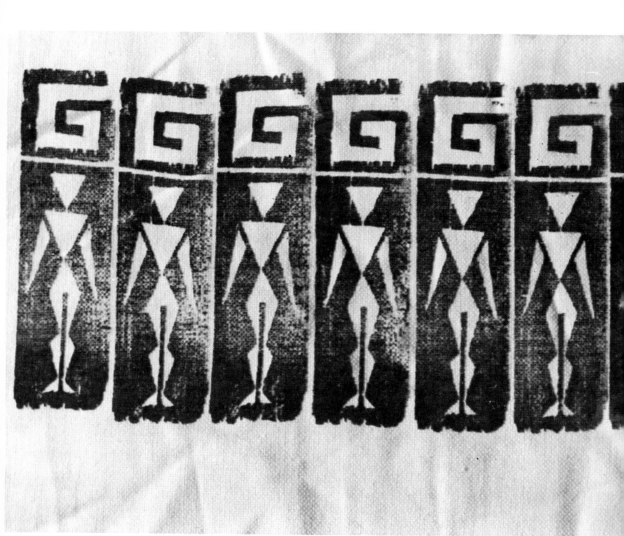

'Greek Motif' (boy, 14). Lino-cut
printed on linen.

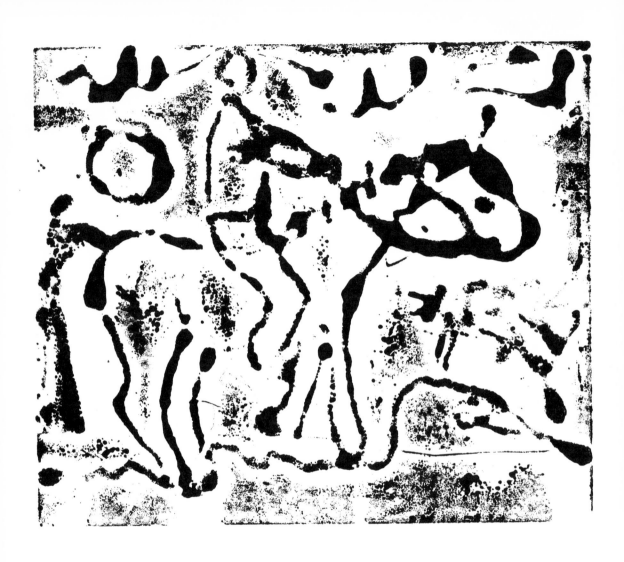

'Horse and Rider' (girl, 13). Print
of a household-cement picture.
For technique, see p. 42.

Index

Table of Technical Skill Levels for Grades 1 through 9

The following table lists the techniques recommended for the various age groups. However, this should not be treated too dogmatically. Here as in all other fields it is found that with suitable guidance children are capable of astonishing achievements. A class of younger children who are encouraged is often creatively and technically more alert than a neglected class of older children. The numbers below indicate the pages where suitable techniques are described.

Grade 1:	6, 7, 8, 9, 10
Grade 2:	6, 7, 8, 9, 10, 16, 42
Grade 3:	6, 7, 8, 9, 10, 11, 16, 21, 23, 42
Grade 4:	6, 7, 8, 9, 10, 11, 12, 13, 15, 16, 21, 23, 35, 36, 42
Grade 5:	6, 7, 8, 9, 10, 11, 12, 13, 14, 15, 16, 17, 18, 21, 23, 24, 25, 28, 29, 31, 33, 35, 36, 42
Grade 6:	6, 9, 10, 11, 12, 13, 14, 15, 16, 17, 18, 19, 21, 22, 23, 24, 25, 26, 27, 28, 29, 30, 31, 32, 33, 35, 36, 37, 41, 42, 43
Grades 7, 8 and 9:	6, 9, 10, 11, 12, 13, 14, 15, 16, 17, 18, 19, 20, 21, 22, 23, 24, 25, 26, 27, 28, 29, 30, 31, 32, 33, 34, 35, 36, 37, 38, 39, 40, 41, 42, 43